ELSEWHERE & BACK

ELSEWHERE & BACK

NEW & SELECTED POEMS

MAIRI MacINNES

BLOODAXE BOOKS

ISBN: 1 85224 199 3

First published 1993 by
Bloodaxe Books Ltd,
P.O. Box 1SN,
Newcastle upon Tyne NE99 1SN.

Bloodaxe Books Ltd acknowledges
the financial assistance of Northern Arts.

Cover printing by J. Thomson Colour Printers Ltd, Glasgow.

Printed in Great Britain by
Cromwell Press Ltd, Broughton Gifford, Melksham, Wiltshire.

for Fergus

Acknowledgements

I should like to thank the editors of the following magazines and anthologies for permission to reprint poems: *The New Yorker, The Tri-Quarterly Review, Prairie Schooner, The Literary Review* (USA), *Massachusetts Review, The Observer, PN Review, P.E.N. New Poetry II* (Quartet, 1988), *Spectator, New Statesman & Society* and *Stand.*

'The House on the Ridge Road' first appeared in the book of that name published in 1988 by the Rowan Tree Press, Boston, together with 'The Old Naval Airfield', 'I Look for Him Everywhere', 'Destruction on the Delaware-Raritan Canal, 1984-1986', 'The Cave-In', and 'Welcome to Mendocino'. 'I Object, Said the Object' appeared in an earlier collection, *Herring, Oatmeal, Milk & Salt* (Quarterly Review of Literature Contemporary Poetry Series, Princeton, New Jersey, 1982).

I should like also to thank wholeheartedly the (US) National Endowment for the Arts, the New Jersey Council on the Arts, the Ingram-Merrill Foundation, the MacDowell Colony, and Yaddo for their help and support.

Contents

III. GULFS

I

HERE

As to incomers, we winter um, and summer um, and winter um again, and then we make up our minds about um.

NORTH COUNTRY SAYING

Die Wahrheit ist das Kind der Zeit, nicht der Autorität.
Truth is the child of time, not the child of authority.

THOMAS MANN

The Return

A right of way marked for a bridle path
leads off the main road into mere brambles,
bracken waist-high, old hawthorn, and a scrub of nettles.
Only the map is encouraging, and the sign of distant banks
with woods in their clefts, and the corroboration
of a stone house over a little valley.
Very well, the path opens into a blackthorn tunnel
and runs a hundred yards spaciously downhill.
But quicken your pace and you'll presently fall,
such is the gloom, where ruts of carts and wagons,
a foot deep, have hardened for over a century
in yellowish clay. And if you push on still
down to the hidden ford and past Ashpole Spinney
across the arable where the path has disappeared,
you'll see, if you're in luck, pencil marks
through the wheat where farm carts passed –
not the ruled line of the main road, stiff as a copy,
but a curve to move you between two hills.

As well be prepared for the shock of arrival.
The green of work in the wood, the green of battle
to come will then grow terribly drab,
as if a bullet fired the moment before
sucked greenness after it, and colour was exhaled
by the gasp of its passage: a thwacked ball,
a brilliant berry fallen from its tree,
a dot of absolute green washed out with a brush.
Why should it bother you? You've come back to your life.
The air of the wood flows lucid and grey like water.
The holly trees glitter. No interlude is perceptible.
Growth-decay-growth rules the appearances.
At the top of the lane the milk tanker changes gear,
the postvan rattles over the cattle grid,
the windscreen of a car glints along the road.
The snowdrops are in place, underneath the drab,
ready to burst out and send you reeling.
You will write your old friends from now on, week by week,
'No trip this year, why don't you come and stay?
Between us we've seen it all. Now let's begin to love.'

Mass

1.

Someone said in a dream, 'Flying's dead easy –
just give yourself to the air.'
It was true: I tripped on a top stair
and took off like a frisbee.
Stairs rivered beneath in the hall's arroyo,
suns flashed through windows,
and I saw that the carpet
approached like a rig of flowered silk
or the leaf canopy of a rain forest –
and I caught at a bough or strut banister
and dropped down unhurt.

Yet unexpectedly the forest
still went past, and how dense,
how weighty and immediate,
the outer world was!
I still floated, I did not exist
minute after minute but in a burst,
all at once, weightless, a rocket
that fired its stars before it fell.

2.

Last night there was rain
after a summer of drought
and mushrooms cropped in old pasture.
Today I met women gathering them,
a line seen far-off climbing the hill,
their faces touched by the October sun,
strung out, stooped, companionable,
mothers and the mothers of mothers,
neighbours from the village.
I hailed them as a newcomer
out on my own, and they rose up
full height and gazed, gentle as giraffes,
and immediately from crammed baskets
offered me mushrooms...weightless
nothing food, food of the dead.
At its moist uncanny touch I felt
the skin on my fingertips to be
no less than the skin of my life,
so heavy and immediate I was,
so dense and full of earth.

Ten in the Morning

The wheatfield's trimmed with poppies, and the drive cuts across it
to where a hall once stood, listed Grade I, nevertheless demolished
overnight twenty years ago after the contents were sold.
Scaffolding of the old life stands: stable block, servants' house,
barns, cottages, rhododendrons concealing a clotted tench pond,
iron gates to the garden, iron railings strung with barbed wire
keeping black and white cows in the park under clumped oaks.
The drive resumes the pleasure principle with the print of horses.
But achieved form and its ethic? Something's been violated.

Now a storm approaches like a car, head-on. Trees turn to coals
that run with flaming green. The drive is a causeway upon the fire.
The sky crumples and smoulders; flash-bulbs in the valley.
Now soft summer rain fills eye-lashes, now green's doused to ash.
Something's been turned aside. What's shifting things here,
why am I peeved, now the sun's out and I can walk dry the two
          miles home?

Ten at Night

The dog's ear's white
    within its flap.
How cold it is,
    this summer night!

How loud it was
    with tractor and mower,
as Ken the farmer
    mowed winter grass,

with John to follow,
    toss and gather,
and cart after cart
    despatched to silo

throughout the day
    around and around
throughout five fields,
    throughout the day.

The last cut in,
    the machines chug off.
The day was deaf.
    We walk the lane

giddied by hush
    in the green-hung air,
by the clarion clear
    moon on the edge.

Below my bedroom
    the fields stretch out
smoother than linen.
    Below walks a woman

not given to smiles,
    grandchild in arms,
the farmer's wife.
    Whatever she feels

yields to her presence.
    The child looks out
from her head height,
    his hand on her face.

An ancient shawl
    enfolds them both.
She glides like a boat
    upon a canal

beneath his weight,
    not shifting him,
not pointing out.
    The long day's work
has made him light.

Soft Fruit

Our lanes turn on the ends of fields –
a legacy of medieval
Danish land tenure, I'm told.
Hence the bends are atrocious –
folly to whip past, as two cars did
at midnight last Saturday,
doing at least eighty –
two blasts of noise and light,
two spasms, pangs, and gone –

except, just over a hump-backed bridge
on the dark and silent bank
one car, upside down,
wheels softly astir
in a stink of burnt rubber –
and answering to flashlights and voices
two faces in the interior
peering out, with silly smiles:
safe, of course, perfectly intact –

in the dark of a bush
surrounded by frightful thorns
two ripe gooseberries hanging,
luscious, asking to be picked.

Objets d'Art

Castle Howard's festive old hulk
lies in open fields like an opera –
twenty-seven bays and a dome,
parapet with urns, and a baroque
pediment upholding three goddesses, one of them Diana.

The holiday crowds arrive from the town,
park cars and buy tickets.
What, tickets to architecture?
To a hulk? To this enormous fountain?
They sit on the lichened stone and stare and fidget,

seeing a roof mobbed with statues and urns:
but something budges too – four
silhouettes pivot – two urns look odd.
Half a dozen peacocks marooned
up there, implausibly high, six blasts of Tyrian colour,

begin to shriek their spoiled terrible cry
and sail off the roof like plates.
Worth a gasp – each famous tail
steering like a rudder, each crested tiny
head upping like a joystick: how straight

and competent they glide to the lawn,
and alight, and bob, and bow, and strut –
worth a laugh, worth a clap.
From tenement roofs in the Bronx, a storm
barely over, one hell-hot night, during a power cut,

sailed lids, empty garbage cans and drums
into a black and flooded street.
No one in sight, but maniacal jeering.
Only a lost car, headlights on
and suddenly awash to the hubs, on a wrong exit

from the throughway, discovered the performance –
things hugely rebounding and plopping
to and fro in the water, lopsided,
then swinging together by chance,
a chorus rolled by the backed up flood, radiantly bobbing.

The Quarry

We thumped across the railway lines
on the way to Scarborough by the Whitby road
last Sunday, in a trek of cars.
The rails dived left, into the weeds,
and suddenly we saw far back
a socket opened in the moorland face,
tall and creamy and lucid as flesh.
And, nearer (once focused), machinery –
stone saws, block and tackle,
scaffold underpinnings, hoppers,
chutes, and family of riddles.
Understanding, I added
a headful of pebbles. So round and graded
and mountainous they came then, tipped
into their huge cones, to clamber up
and be polished by and shoved:
in the radiant resonant places
quarries were, always, warm even in rain,
a resort for picnics, on ancient wet Sundays
my brother's, since the age of seven.

O that default of his, dazzling with
hardness and fastness – the way-in
dredging its pebbles through bodies laid
laughing and sprawled on each summit,
each cone in its shifting held weighty
and balanced beneath us, pebble islands
trapped inside collar and pocket –
their touch as cold and funny as hands –
and the rush and topple of descent
following, the king stride to the ground!

Already I knew of a world he'd vanish
into, that strawhaired genius
of quarries. Didn't we drive him back
past esplanades and the Grand Hotel
to the dim porch of the school
and leave him? – then set off home,
the headlights sifting batches
of moorland till the quarry flashed by
to make me content – the rest
fobbed off, misplaced,
not even a catch in the breath
to echo someone's sob.

Evening on the Estuary, Noon at Sea

(for Esteban Vicente, painter)

The estuary is violet
   among its reeds and bars.
The field of the evening holds
   in the crown of the sky.
It's dark on the bare hills.
   Ash drifts thick in mile-wide smears
far out at sea – drift emptying content
   where the long waves disappear:

And I remember riding out of Orkney
   on the ferry to Scrabster –
three tides meeting, and a buckling ship;
   tumult and froth below;
aloft, gull-escorted mast and the brave flags.
   It was midsummer in the far north,
the air very bright,
   the wind hard at work –
so much haled out of the fabric of matter
   and tuned like matter, luminous,
excited by present arrival in Caithness.

Here, as darkness fills out,
   absolute circumstance also
begins to bloom.
   The colours of land and water
grow deep in reflected light.
   Here and in your painting, Master,
what's allowed will happen.
   The eye arrives alone at its centre,
its eventual passion.

The Old Naval Airfield

I looked out Henstridge lately,
    somewhere where it always was,
even then, without maps or signs,
    and thought of Philip, chief flying instructor,
brave Philip, who soon was dead –
    long ago, though, many years ago.
Pretty old, bosky old, footpath
    country, and nothing was familiar
till suddenly the dull lane
    roused me. A humpbacked bridge
over a disused railway led me
    to B Camp that was: now a wood and a shed.
Opposite, the Wessex Grain Company –
    storage silos that hummed
in the afternoon air like planes.
    On the edge of the field, a bunker gradually
took my eye. A well-turfed barrow?
    No, dear God, the rusted roof of a hangar
half-fallen in! And over the field, look,
    Philip's control tower, a tall wreck
marooned in breaking waves of grass!

Survival is a form of murder.
    My father ran round the garden in the dark
shouting, 'She's dead, and I could've
    done more for her. I could have, and I didn't.'
She'd said earlier, 'He couldn't do more,
    that man, best man who ever lived.'
Truth is, you can always do more.
    You have to survive, that too, but it's murder.
He lived on, as you do if you can.

Firs

The fir plantation
kept by the Forestry Commission
could be in Russia –
with its aroma of pine,
its loamy mushroom floor,
the ant hills, fir seedlings and birch
on the deep mossy verges,
the walkers' ritual
exchanges of greeting
and the trapped atmosphere.
But pad the path to the outskirts
where mother beeches rustle
in the moorland wind
and huge clouds born of ocean
plane in over Yorkshire
from lakeland and fell –
it's unmistakable
where you are.
The gated road after all
leads down to the valley
of tourist towns, great houses,
the office of information.

Forty Years in a Moorland Parish
i.m. Rev. J.C. Atkinson (1814-1900)

Men shot the great spotted woodpecker
oftentimes out of Parson's wood.
What with shooting, the parson writes,
and felling of trees, 'the visits to the wood
of those harmless interesting beautiful
birds became strangely like angels'.'
What was the code for anger?

Guns also took out of his district
the glorious kingfisher and the barn owl,
the merlin, of course, and the kestrel.
As for the multitude of rooks,
magpies, chaffinches, cuddies, thrushes, robins –
summer saw many of them cut down
by the husbandman with his shotgun.

What the code was for anger, Parson didn't know.
He often took his own gun to the moors,
and yet put crumbs upon his windowsill
to feed his 'starving bird pensioners',
always wondering, indeed marvelling
at the rare and ever rarer woodpecker
that still came like an angel.

A Writer's Tale

Dawn. Stove dead as a stone. Windows bleared.
But a damp sheet of paper on the table
covered with words he was surely incapable of –
such passion, such persuasion they had,
he said in awe – embers of a late stint
that left him dropping on the narrow cot,
exhaustion covering him like an old quilt.
The kindest of smiles as he looked up
and told this tale, and rain dried on the road,
seas gleamed across the point, and
his famous hut stood there by the wood
for the world to see – for them, especially –
friends at the big-house window, glass in hand.
He said as if ashamed: 'Then came this bonus –
through a port-hole wiped on the glass
of my lonely hut, a vixen and her cubs
appeared stalking, ambushing, frisking,
in plain sight among the leaves and grass,
as I used to see them when I was a boy.
I could have wept – no, no, no, no,
not out of boastfulness, out of humility.'

And yet the listening friend found him a fraud –
in foxes and words, outrageously impudent.
In time, though, equipped with a workroom too
at last, what did she find herself? – a terrier
snorting and rolling on the icy grass,
hollies roof-high glittering in the wind,
hellebores' fans and frills that grew
out of dead beech leaves by the workroom wall,
green and whitish-green petals, translucent
like pond ice or the wax tip of a lit candle:
not foxes, however, nor delphic words
tapped out by a typewriter – less oracular
things than her words she couldn't imagine,
but gravely sure of themselves, and even critical
of her, that vessel they would empty and fill
with their own worth, over and over again,
till it was a joke, or ceremony of innocence
at which she sometimes cried, like a mother at a wedding.

The Man from Principle
(for Robin Hildyard)

Simple and necessary
is the path on the ridge
that grew there long ago and stayed;
the fields and woods below no less,
and the stone house
nested in their midst,
growing twelve chimneys
slow as oaks

and the painter on the path
is simple and necessary too,
this morning in August,
with easel, palette, brush,
sunburnt, in old shorts and shirt,
tormented with thunder bugs;
the convener of so much:
masses, squares, diagonals,
in emeralds, ochres, duns,
woods impasto, pasture wash, wheat splash,
and the dear square blob of the house,
the same that would house
this landscape of itself
upon the inward of a painted wall,
vacant, in clear possession.

But a half-truck bumps up.
It's battered, blue, familiar.
Two dwarf terriers bark
noiseless behind the cab glass.
The farmer climbs out,
the man from principle,
cold guardian of the scene,
whose address is anger.
His voice is a horn:
'What's become of manners?'
'*What?*' 'You could have asked permission,
before you started to paint.'

'*Permission, on a right of way?*'
'It would have been good manners.
But where are manners, these days, I ask?'

He brings her to order, he thinks,
though it's order she's brought:
here it is, on the canvas.
He rides over all she paints or says,
a huntsman with contradictions
baying around his feet.
Such manners as he mourns,
when did they exist?
She is dumbfounded.
When the painting hangs in the house,
we try to grasp it, grasp it.

II

THERE AND THEN

Nature is what we know.

EMILY DICKINSON

The House on the Ridge Road
An Imaginary History

1. *Midwinter, New England*

Snow flies through the ribs of the barn
caught like an elk in its thicket
till nothing remains but bone

snow out to inhabit
its delicate derelict house
tipped into a dark wood
lidding the cold chimney
blanking the door   blinding the window
wadding the carriage lane
humping box hedge and rose bush
letting a single white line
unroll between wood and torpid grey light
where cars pass

snow out to penetrate
that broken space where the orchard survives
in front   on crutches
where apple trees are elbow deep
on white tussocks stitched with straw

The long white corridor of the ridge road
flicks past as quick as a marble
The empty house bobs quietly away
leaning into the snow of the rear mirror
a woman in white waving and running
then stopping and looking after me.

2. *What They Say Happens*

The mother of us all is queening it there.
She is for ever sweeping the floor.
A fire of apple logs is burning:

logs of pearmain, russet, pippin –
they blaze on the hearth and puff apple breath
at a row of huddled children.

Their hands are warming like small cold stars.
The mustiness from closed windows and doors
has vanished up the chimney.

The snow windows are full of the snow field
and coils of apple smoke unwrapping over it
and over the road where a woman wantonly stares.

The winter wind snaps smoke out like a sheet.
Strips melt into the dark of the woods,
bending the light, spreading the smell of apples.

The house creaks inside, opening like a wooden flower.
The narrow staircase shudders with delight
as our mother throws the bones
of yet another apple tree upon the fire.

3. *What In Fact Happened*

The walls unwrap, the roof pays out shingles,
the chimney shifts its coping, the doorstep founders.
The past reveals its core,
the hard brown pips, the apple future.

Once, deep in another house,
a man doffed his hat and a servant took it –
a worn old hat, soft and black,
exuding dirt and experience.

He stood bare-headed in the parlour
in the attitude of arrival.
(His arrival was not yet spent;
his horse's hoofbeats sounded in his ear.)
The royal home-filled lady of the house
sat down in a gilt pin-legged chair
and her dress composed itself about her
(greenish it was, leafy flounces
and lacy white ruffles sheathing her feet).

He pressed forward into the occasion,
his hands riding hard on his knees,
his boots shedding mud on the figured carpet.
He presented her with an account of himself.
It made a medallion – on one side
the clerical father in black
and the grey-eyed sister and her lover
with crow-winged eyebrows and air of nobility;
and the splendid apple orchard
that was theirs, extending to the river;
on the other, himself,
the runaway boy who'd taken ship
to a small disorderly country at war.
A soldier of fortune he'd become,
with gun and tattered uniform,
brown, skeletal, foxy,
a dodger among rocks in upland country,
who'd laid waste countrysides
through twelvemonth campaigns,
and pillaged, and plundered.

He did not say what else –
whether he'd fathered children
and they'd died, or if he murdered.

Later he brought home the booty of two kingdoms,
and the knowledge of how to live on roots and mice.
At times he'd gone mad, and he knew it.
But he'd hushed the grand adjuring voices

(those in Scripture, those in the mouths
of friars and missionaries).
He watched himself suffer instead.

The supernatural wildness in him roared like a fire.

But the lady heard also a child's voice,
a solace craving to work itself out
as sap drops from the grape vine in the spring;
child Adam, his kiss at the ready,
eyebright in the tangle of the meadow,
waiting to be born:

while the man spoke of his darling,
the daughter of the house, and of betrothal.

The man deep in his account of himself.
The lady considering the medallion.
Her hands nesting in her silken lap.
With the ebb and flow of her breath,
the house rose up off its foundations
and rode with her, and
necessity began to float free.
Unity was moving up minute by minute,
movement hauled to its stop,
the doors of a wound coming together and healing;
the daughter venturing over her own sill
for the first time, and stooping and lighting the fire.

4. *A Desire*

Warming in large pale hands:
the blossom of small cold feet.

Tightshut child eyes, heldbreath kiss:
russet apple flesh bite.

Child whispers:
dry apple leaves shifting on grit.

Child weight on lap:
a man's great fruit.

5. *The Settlement*

But not yet. First a gash in the scalp of the land,
    its gold brown hair ripped back,
maple trunks piled and picked clean.
    The discarded roots, the burning stocks.
Extracted roots and their sockets.
    The lurching of men, the lurching of yoked oxen.
The fires, the smoke, the trampling, the mud.

The cries of men, the creaking of harness.
The smell of new-cut seasoned timber.
    The burr of the saw, the chut of the adze.

From the town below, smoke perceived on the ridge.

Later, the great stones formed cellar walls,
    enclosing a space instead of occupying it,
and the floor was laid over the cellar space,
    so the house began to rest on the bottom of its word
and to rise gradually out of it,
    darkening the word, estranging it, becoming wooden,
hollow, the hollow heart of a tree.

6. *The Daily Round*

The farm ticked
to the heart clock
asleep, dark
awake, light
at dawn, work

wood a flame
and leaf a tongue
and stone a coat

on a feather bed
they floated nightly
over the apple trees

7. *The Summoning of the Children*

A homeless past. Nothing with a name.
    Empty eggshell words blowing about,
clumping and trickling in front of the feet.
    Flat land, dull sky, stationary river.
Temperate climate, lack of the seasons.
    Nothing to remember.

Mother led them out. They came through a wood
  to a new place where everything had a name.
'This is your heart,' she said, 'this is your head,
  and this is the third kingdom between them
where your house is and your orchard,
  and your mind and your heart are at one.'
They ran about under the apple trees
  and sang the songs that were waiting to be sung.

> *The apple trees stand still today*
>   *But they won't stand forever.*
> *All night long they'll dance and sing*
>   *At the coming of April weather*

and

> *Bear, bear, you apple trees,*
>   *Red and green and yellow*
> *Bear, bear, you apple trees,*
>   *My master won't let you lie fallow.*

Mother stayed with them always. They watched her,
  for they feared she'd be forfeit because of them
and have to return to the anonymous region.
  The eldest boy made up this song:

> *When I'm a man I'll build you a house*
> *Of applewood and see-through glass*
> *And I'll put you in it and live with you*
> *And you'll never die but I will too.*

'Why,' grumbled the mother, 'the moment you're grown
  you'll be off and running like a set of hares,
leaving me all alone. I tell you this:
  though you think you cannot bear to lose me now,
it'll be your father you'll dote on then –
  though he doesn't give you a thought today
except when he falls over you and your toys.'
  And immediately they felt their first doubts;
and after their surprise, they began to laugh.

The world's candle is lit (they sang)
The world's candle is lit!
O foolish Mother, to think that you can
Lie to us even a bit!

8. *The Groundhog*

Dark: a grinding and gnawing.
Leprous buildings coming alight.
Stink of blood.

Click of the ready: ratchet of the clock,
scurry and plink of a blind going up.

On the grass by the barn, a working, a lump:
rawhead and bloodybones.
And when the gun went off, pandemonium.

Something hurried to the wall
dragging its heavy furs.
Out of a door at a run, thick with desire
for its ancient barbarous flesh,
its huge teeth, its stupidity,
the man caught it, clubbed it till it was limp,
humped it to the wall
and dumped it over. Back in the kitchen
the house dog nosed his hand.
The children pointed: 'Blood! Blood!'
as he took off his boots. Fear,
fear and laughter made them choke.

As they wheezed and screamed, he felt again
tremors in his fingertips where the dog's tongue worked,
beast sighs in their small pink mouths,
hatred in their wrong hysteria.

9. *The Man, His Orchard, His Bees, His Children*

Every spring the man set out his beehives
    along the orchard runways –
neat white bee houses,
    hangars for his bombers,
his humming honey droppers
    in their ancient papal uniform
of striped old blonde and starlight brown
    and black black legs.

Old soldier that he was,
    his blood kindled to his bees'
delirious dance on the scouts' return,
    the dance of bee muses inspiring apples,
ho hum ho hum as they undid
    the coded bales of air;
then heavy lift-off on short chopper wings,
    soaring over trees in flower
and homing laden with nectar.
    Adieu as the squads moved out!
Laughter at the thought
    of their gingering up stamens
with the ginger gold dust on their thighs,
    and the grateful love milk of nectar!

Their continual bee rage,
    the violence of their passion in his ear,
charged him with exaltation.
    He heard strong flames licking the pit
through which the Christ child stormed
    on his way to spring time's prisoners;
the god burning in his throat,
    Jeremiah's wrath, vengeful Apollo's.

To own an orchard was no small thing –
    to be paradise's renter.
O lovely enmity of bees there!
    Their honey and fruiting business!
The wild prickers lodged
    in blundering human flesh,
poor little bees dying to the full,
    abandoned bee corpses empty as air!

Death's bee sting, now –
    its stiff little footnote
to the blossoming text of the orchard –
    if he took it into account,
his simple being might suffice
    as an event. He trembled at the thought.
He wanted to live for ever
    in the douce haven of the orchard.
He dismantled centuries of deprivation.
    He let them drop and fall over,
old vessels that leaked quietly
    into the ground and lost even their names.
The earth absorbed them and became different;
    it looked sometimes like the Old Country.
But here he was master. Go, bees, he ordered.
    (His invented life appalled him –
the rawness of it, its complacency.)

Hard headed, though, he knew
    the orchard was to be understood,
not to be reasoned out.
    It was dirt to be rubbed in the eyes.
He was to take it as a report
    about things taking their course
as usual, about a farm's continuities;
    a letter sent to a son at the front,
a homesick soldier. So the man thought.

A rush of dead children.
    The father furious in the orchard
flailing the blossom,
    killing the sacred bees.

10. *Lament for the Children*

Where are they off to
so early, the moment it's light?
Where are they off to?
Their kidding and laughter
last night filled the orchard
like tumultuous water
chuckling and splashing
under the keel of a ship.

Where are they off to
in their best? It isn't Sunday –
where are they off to
in their floating white dresses
and serious suits,
young men and women,
flower of the orchard
cut from a hundred boughs?

Where are they off to?
The ridge road is empty.
Where are they off to?
They've gone to fetch winter,
its frosts and gale winds,
to put out the fires
and wrench open windows
and let snow drift on the stair.

11. *A Retreat*

The weekly garbage truck
pants up the hill
trailing a smell of midden
Two men
hang on its shoulders
They discharge themselves
up driveways
over snowy lawns
Staggering they return
hefting coloured bins
They fire them
into the bunker
of the moaning truck

Freak messages of rot

12. *How It May End*

The man's end might be cleaner cut than hers,
a name speaking up out of survey or tax record,
his marginalia in a shelf of books, his look
cropping up in a dozen descendants' faces,
a path he trod through a wood
that never made it into highway
or was quite overgrown,
and a rapt place on a street
where on a summer night he was caught by an air
played in a single bright room of a neighbouring house
with a woman at the piano and a boy on a flute;
he saw and heard, and was taken up through the dark
in pleasure; so much so his wife thought
afterward how much she'd missed,
as if he hadn't already embodied her regret,
on her lips a recollected touch,
a bit rough like a Russet,
a bit smooth like a Red Delicious.

She called her neighbours rootless, though,
creatures of a mimic life,
they were so plainly out to laugh
as they swerved to avoid her,
stalwart on the crown of the old ridge lane,
booted like a seaman, cuffed with grey socks,
skirt and cardigan hitched with a pin,
eyes intent under the ancient tam,
her senses seized in the old house,
like paper at exit from a door, torn off.
Birds migrated throughout her mind
and she barely noticed – she didn't have to,
her own end never anywhere in sight.
She lay down in traffic now and then
to call attention to the rotten state of the world.
She muttered through town meetings – they knew her well.

When her gaze swivelled at last, she knew
they'd driven past with their understanding
hugged to their secret heart –
down with relief into driveways
tight between boulder and boulder,
shouldering thinned out trees, nursers of a view.
There they kindly thought of her as answer
to questions that wouldn't come up.
Babies had been born in her bed, hadn't they?
There too the dead had lain, immensely admired.

The neighbours were frivolous, however;
preoccupied with infinity,
its clean floors and diamond ceilings.
Whatever she embodied they laid aside
like a photograph or a tea-cloth freshly ironed
for the last time.

13. *A Memory of Girlhood in the Other Country*

Still on the snow lane
packed by its tyre prints
she thought of the journey home
over the hills by train

after staying with Margaret
when she was ten –
clear-shot fields, tops white as lint,
bottoms of ash and oak

hammered with snow strokes,
a durable script;
no sound but the engine;
alone in her carriage,

lonely, nothing to read,
only now and then at a halt
the cheerful guard
enquiring how she was,

until the train slid
into her station, a vast sleeve
of gauzy glare and steam
in which her father waited.

When they drove home
through flash of bike
and tram and car and rig
that edged through a sparkling dark

she told how Margaret
had a delightful family
in the house beyond the hills
surrounded by its woods and fields;

some days they'd sledded
and spent some on ponies afield;
they made up wild games each night
and whispered tales in bed.

At last the train, good little flunkey,
ran her home over the fells.
And now she saw herself
a pair of travelling eyes

observing a piecemeal land
finally one; beyond reach,
and so pure she ached;
because she couldn't join it, sad.

And she went quiet for lack of words.
She looked inward
and felt the train still moving
and saw the fell again and heard
murmuring within her skull
stone, hill, snow, girl.

14. *A View in Winter*

One day soon after I returned
the elm on the ridge went down
snow-clotted till it tumbled.
A dish of dark roots in the air –
the mare rolled in the field
just so last summer, flaunting
her dark rose-spackled belly,
kicking her dark grey legs until
she staggered up and veered
over the orchard wall, to gorge
on apples, her just reward.

After the fall the elm groans
deep in itself, relieved of its weight
as it settles, cracking and creaking,
moving into itself, into its heart
until it's at ease this once
with the muffling vast unsurpassable snow.

Now It's Over

Cut off in that remote Berlin,
    the second Christmas of our marriage –
        thirty-six years ago, this was –

we dreamed of an escape to Austria
    and, passports stamped, complete with Russian visa,
        drove from expensive shops and operatic ruins

into a horizontal undreamt-up country,
    other Germany, supposed to live with less.
        We thought of seeing smoking chimney-pots

belonging to some farm; of cows, and sheep,
    and someone fetching hay across the snow;
        and country birds: a pheasant, or a crow.

In fact, the plain stretched clean as a sheet,
    and the autobahn, quite young, unworn,
        lay dead on its back. For miles nothing stirred

until a horse and cart appeared on a bridge
    clear of the field, far-off, a bleb
        on the white, a barely moving bleb.

And so what difference could we make? –
    a couple with a year-old baby
        crammed into an Isetta, two-stroke

bubble runabout, bright red for pluck,
    out to fool no one – yet we were *traffic*
        at the barriers met every thirty miles,

where soldiers tumbled out to look us over,
    jamming fur hats deeply over brows,
        muffled, buttoned, booted, shouldering

guns, smelly, raw-chapped, unshaved,
    but curious, and eager. After they
        surveyed our papers, before they waved

us through, there were some tender moments –
   (not for the baby): *how fast did it go,*
      our motorcycle car, our pram?

What mileage did we get? And last,
   shameless, *How much did it cost?*
      They thought, and kicked the tyres. *Not much!*

So – going to the Alps? Why not?
   And when they sniffed and smiled, and gave a sort
      of shrug. *One day, huh?* We barely understood.

On the Bridge at Salamanca
(for Priscilla Barnum)

At the far end of the bridge and out of sight
there is a tremendous clatter
of horses. Then there's silence.
A man shouts, and there's another clatter.
It is strange how they hesitate,
till again we hear that frightful shout.
And now as we raise our heads and peer,
the horses fizz up, and we scatter,
barrelling flesh shoves us against the parapets –
the bridge is old and narrow and very long –
something the Romans left – and so
we have nowhere to run to, none of us,
we are so many, perfect strangers,
city people, not used to herd animals,
or such bright flesh and huge glassy bosses
of eyes or reckless squashing past.

They are not remotely like painted horses
given to marching·on church walls,
all natural piety and acquiescence!
We are amazed by their acrid smell,
and then by their surge of strength,
and their mysterious see-saw, like rocking horses;
though now we see the horses are hobbled;
a two-foot chain between the fore-legs
limits each stride to a hop
or burlesque high-heeled waggle.
And so we smile, how can we not smile!
They look after all quite silly.

The burly herdsman is angry;
he shouts impatiently and waves his stick –
for the crowds delay the passage of his horses.
At the very end of the bridge he waits:
the horses lurch down a bank to their pasture
under the high trees by the river,
and lower their heads and start to graze.

Relieved, amused, we look from the parapet.
Beside the horses, under an awning
stretched between bank and pole,
a baby and a girl are fast asleep,
fast, fast asleep on mattresses.
The herdsman leaves, first thwacking a tree.
The horses after all are hobbled.
The children are quite safe – 'Gypsies,'
someone remarks with satisfaction.
Can it be right, to use the open air
like a house? Is it entirely safe?
The horses hop at random, grazing,
drinking from the river, careless,
spreading out further and further.

Destruction on the Delaware-Raritan Canal, 1984-1986

The dredgers jounced out on their juggernauts
    leaving the old clogged canal cut loose
from hundreds and hundreds of trees; reeved, skimmed, taut,
    useful fresh water between scrubbed embankments;
and the lake was revealed, and sky, and rim of land;
    and I saw for the first time how canal ran to mill
squat by the weir where the lake fell in a line;
    and how it proceeded to the quarry rock
newly visible on the horizon, where (said reason)
    cargoes awaited lading as at the mill
on strings of barges headed for New York.
    Cube, line, cone: geometry of need
obscured till now by wealth of tree.
    So much I murmured, observing from the bridge,
hearing a plainer message than the one I used to,
    in winter, when greys of sky and lake mingle anyway,
and the towpath is barely a smudge beyond the reeds.

Come spring, I halt there stunned when I arrive on foot
    at the lock to take the path that once ran under trees
and follow the old water road, old cut between rivers,
    and find nothing to speak to me and nothing to hear.
This is the resolution of an interrogation room
    which leaves a towpath gum studded with stumps
and hundreds of tree stocks piled on the silt,
    rings of their age exposed in the lab of air,
while light beats down its unstoppable repetitions:
    what for? and *who?* and *how?* in smashing silence.
How bitterly I recall the familiar couplet lines
    of oak and cherry, black-flowered ash, red-flowered maple,
walnut; the calligraphy of ivy and bramble,
    the messenger birds, the Ariadne butterflies,
and flower illuminations, and oarsmen's Morse flashes
    that signalled through the camouflage of leaves;
and the five white heron contacts in midstream
    last summer, that floated up into the trees
on my approach, and hung there like sheets of music, a folio
    for eyes only, to sound only in auricles of mind!
Nearer town maples remain, green tokens, every thirty yards.

O maples, singletons, humming in the wind
like telegraph poles, that used to be great swaying choruses! –
    isn't it betrayal, simply to survive?
Let the wind tear into each tree and branches crack
    and sparks of red flowers ignite and flare on the path –
they are electric, merely, kisses on metal.
    What if grass flares over the banks and mallards nest beneath? –
I come to them churched out, musing and mourning,
    the canal my Bosphorus; it flows full of the dead.

Yet the water ruffles in harmony over canal and lake,
    the path between them runs smooth, free of roots and stones,
ideal for runners, who throng here, at odds with implication,
    leaving aside what isn't theirs, running without looking,
the mould into which they're poured ready to be knocked out.
    I notice the moustache of one soft on his lip, his hair
brown too, and wavy; he dodges past at speed,
    an irruption from a world he affirms but does not see.
It's sweet to see him race, to feel thrust on to an old
    level of myself, outside my time, away from my own ends.
What made him as he is, I wonder: did his mother
    sit at the airport cold and dispassionate
like some old goddess the day he flew out for ever?
    He's like the Achilles Homer tells us of
in the Iliad, who with the death of Patroclus his lover
    at the hands of Hector ran amok among the Trojans.
Achilles killed so many the river burst its banks in rage
    and tried to drown him. The waves were so dangerous
a god sent fire; tamarisk and willow and elm
    burst into flame along the banks and miles of reed beds burned,
till the river was chastened and turned back. Achilles got off
    and lived to hunt down Hector. Afterwards
the land must have looked pretty much like this – tree stumps,
    mud, oblivious runner tearing out of sight.

The arithmetic of distance starts to tick,
    the wind falls, and in place of rain, ersatz
tears for dead Hector or the savaged land or all there is –
    pockmarks on the flow, followed by a calm
in which the light gathers and spreads over the water,
    a sheet stretched taut, collapsed, drawn taut, as no doubt then.

Among the Sea Islands, Georgia

A half-completed island, this:
Mud and marsh lapse into salt water
on the landward side, while
on the coast facing the open sea,
beaches run clean and straight,
forming the original sand spit,
and the land rises from it dark
with grassland and woods.
So the track along the spine
is half shell, half soil.
Palm and pine grow side by side,
palmetto lying in between like old
wrecked basket chairs,
and there are stands of venerable
evergreen oak, hung with Spanish moss
like ancient flags in a cathedral.
Woods pare off at the end
to the white quick of sand.
Here skeletons of whole trees
lie beached like ships,
and hoofprints, delicate shells,
loop in from the dunes: first signs of life.
A dredging sea, with loons and porpoises
fishing, far out; but the creek nearby
lies furred, killed off
by run-offs from brown tannic pools.

Of all who lived here once
to raise their sugar cane and rice,
no man remains, and little else.
Vanished, the lot – the paddy fields,
great house, huts, wharf,
warehouses, whipping blocks.
Only milestones in woods are left,
pointing to lost plantations,
and the gravestones of 'Lottie', 'Tib'.
How sad, somehow, it is,
this scrupulous lack of consequence!

What if the spring now lets fall
its present like a canticle,
and the snakes coil warming in the path,
or that painted bunting
flits like a pentecostal flame
in and out of a bush?
The boatman does not care.
He checks his fine gold watch
and says it's time to go.
A squall is coming. We cannot wait.
Nothing to be done but this.
Nothing matters now.

At Five the Train

At five the train left Hendaye
and trundled inland, across
the foothills of the Pyrenees,
bound for Marseille.

At dusk it drew up somewhere,
earth dark, horizon high,
a greenness in the air,
and stars over the hills.

Half the passengers dismounted,
and doors slammed on crowds.
That's how we knew it was Lourdes,
that and the little fires
carried up under the stars.

We sat in the dark carriage,
broke bread and drank wine,
until we couldn't see
what was flame and what star,
and the train took us off to Marseille
in secret, as before.

III

GULFS

Au moral comme au physique, j'ai toujours eu la sensation du gouffre, non seulement du gouffre du sommeil, mais du gouffre de l'action, du rêve, du souvenir, du désir, du regret, du remords, du beau, du nombre, etc...

BAUDELAIRE

(Morally and physically, I have always been conscious of the gulf, not only the gulf of sleep, but the gulf of action, dreams, memory, desire, regret, remorse, the beautiful, numbers, etc...)

Camping in Winter
(for Antoinette)

Your morning comes like the flash at the end of the world,
as will tomorrow morning, and the one after that,
and you'll be caught by it repeatedly.
You'll not learn to anticipate it, not quite yet,
but view it always amazed through the crack of your lids:
the immaculate sky blotting you out with light;
more and more light glancing obliquely at you
from white mountain parted by white glacier;
nothing dark except your hair, the dirt on your hands,
the blue of your sleeping bag,
always amazing because you've accepted nothing.

My morning accumulates, one apparition after another.
The window's enough to coat each thing with light.
The ceiling sways as if the street's in flood,
but it's cars passing, reflecting dabs of light.
Shadows pale into the thick mat of the page,
the one I work on, the blank you don't yet love,
lit by the clarity of your absence.
Now in the current of this daily existence
without secrets or colours or noise
you begin to take hold. Recognised, you start and laugh.
Your lips and cheeks flush, your eyes and hair darken.
I'm running to meet you, blind with light,
just as, replenished, you speed out,
a mark on the brilliance, a tall girl
skiing across the snowfield with her pack.

I Object, Said the Object

Out of the habit, I remembered nothing,
   Till, like a drunkard beating on the door,
   She shrieked out, 'More!' and more
      She had to have.
It was our anniversary. The devil longed
For rings and songs and coloured rocks and tinsel.

I wish the police would fix her.
   They'd end her screams with an axe's chop.
   What bliss to hear that yell lopped off!
      Think of the blank
Flowering, and then her coiffed acquaintance
Relishing her visceral history and sad finis.

I wonder now just how I could have picked her.
   Liable, was she reward? Her loss leucotomy?
   Was she the fundamental shifting at the eye
      Of penetrating pain?
Do magical mischances falter without her, the needle
In vision, for earth to pivot on, like an apple?

Whatever she meant once, appreciation's over.
   Today was bad. Tomorrow will be worse.
   Some hormone malady has made her haggish,
      Storming the stairs,
Mouth agog to the quivering uvula,
Taut hands like blown-up gloves waggling disaster –

Day after day I send for the doctor,
   And let his hollow needle intercept the kill.
   Thankfully I watch the boggling congeal,
      The blubbering less.
Sobered, she recovers rapidly,
Her eyes awash like two great silly puddles.

And then she swears she's never loved me more.
   She takes me in her big caress,
   Delicate diva, apt to bless,
      Hand on my head,
As if through blubbing we grow richer and closer,
Instead of always poorer and more cold.

But soon high-horsed again, she hops away,
   And sorry that I've let her be ridiculous,
   And slow to monkey with the maladress
      That she displays,
I let her bolt and wander, and play herd
Upon the unsteady spending of her miscellaneous powers.

So it may happen, some night noble and serene,
   The last phut firework of her endeavour done,
   She'll turn, sane, cool, and say, 'Come,
      Bring down your sheep.
November's leaning on the fells, and Cassiopeia
Leans down to chant her song. Count your last lambs.'

Heart-full and grateful then I'll bid them come,
   Their mouths like filmstars' ravaged and remote
   Uttering sounds unchosen, spontaneous, not
      Chidden, flocking,
My lambs, crowding to me, a stranger that says,
'What is it that you want? Is it this? Or this?'

The Fields of Light

Again and again, a presence in the clearing
    that was the clearing itself;
the row of firs in snowy quilts,
    the parting of sky and snow.
Again and again the cold unpainted room,
    the dead fire, the tap's needle of cold,
the cooling skins of the bed, the kettle's fuss,
    the bang and commotion of the furnace.
Twigs kindled, waggling fingers of warmth.
    The days began by writing themselves.
Dark words ploughed the fields of light.

In the afternoons, in the riding barn,
    old William waited: twenty years old,
plump in his baize winter coat,
    ancient and patient and horse. Round and round
the riding barn among the competent
    petulant well-mounted little girls
thumped William, reliable Pegasus
    for the reliable winter poet.
Later, blown, the unsaddled William
    examined his stall, munched hay, propped a hoof.
He may have remembered Homeric gallops,
    leaps, falls, great treks home in rain
after getting lost, long miles from home;
    or that was the poet, steering a metal vehicle
back to the rented cabin in the woods.

On the very last day, the firs written up,
    the snow, the fires, the light and dark,
and William, all caught and bound,
    the poet drove out of the clearing in the trees
to where the route for the city
    zippered up the divided woods,
the fields of snow, the icy marshes,
    the great lovely vistas opened down valleys.

But a mile or two out, there was William
    entering the highway from a country lane
at full gallop, riderless, tail high as a flag,
    two silly colts along, a band of marauders
drunk with merriment, that sent the traffic
    braking, parking, flashing hazard lights
while elementary horseplay went on –
    such bucking and cavorting, squeals and nips!
A poet could scarcely believe it.

Then, rapture spent, William permitted a running girl
    to catch up, and submitted to a halter
and so walked home to the barn, the colts
    trotting obediently at heel – but not before
he had let out a neigh like a clarion
    and produced a prodigious buck, to show
the drivers edging into the flow of traffic
    how unreliable he was, how original,
how easily he broke the dark lines
    the poet had laid over the fields of light.

To a Dachshund

Brown buck of a dog,
    why wince when I put down my hand?
I've just pulled a tick
    off your ruched lip,
six off your lappet ear.
    I've bathed a sore pad
before now, swilled out an eye,
    freed jaws jammed on a bone.
In late hot August, without fail,
    I drive you to shallow water;
there you wade to the eyes,
    your tail swishes –
sometimes you shove off
    and become a crocodile.
When you surge out,
    your mask wrinkles with laughter.
In early March
    I escort you to the fields
when they first stir with mice
    and rabbit kittens
pop about the path.
    You thunder after them,
immodest as a horse.
    You've never caught one,
and yet I cheer
    your swaggering return.
Why then do you cringe
    as the wing of my palm descends?
True, you soon recover yourself.
    Your black eye swivels
to the cushion beside me,
    your dot brows flash.
A lighthouse
    couldn't be clearer.
Let's get it straight, friend:
    you live like an emperor.

Still, brown dog, your bullyhood,
    your fidgets and snores,
yes, even how you smell,
    will speak to my oldest dreams
so long as you allow,
    say, once a day,
my hand to confirm your pelt
    is warm and soft as bread,
your dense musculature
    nests thick as rope
over those stout legs
    like furniture, but wrinkled:
my hand so hankers after
    your indifferent bones;
it wants to know
    its hoped-for partner,
that other hand
    inside the puppet glove.

The Tympanist

After the full-bodied roar of the street
the recital hall looks extravagantly useless
to the first of us filing in
to be chilled by the cold off the iron pillars,
the echo in the coved enormous ceiling,
the brilliance of the crystal chandeliers.
The more people come in, however, the more the air
thickens and grows moist, as if we brought
vapours and warmth with us from the street.
See how the earliest are by now at home,
secure in their seats and beginning to breathe easy:
we put on our glasses to thumb through a programme
and stare at the platform where at the rear
the tympanist is going through his remarkable ceremony.
What is he doing, exactly, bending his ear
over the biggest drum as if it murmured
to the delicate ear-drum inside his own skull?
And what is he doing now, placing a hand
over the vellum of the next tub?
Is he shutting it up, is he tuning it,
his four digits and thumb outrider
touching it lightly, stilling its vibrations?
There are three of these drums as well as some cymbals.
Each septum is taut, and he listens at each,
until with a grimace he looks up and reveals
his bone mask, frightful, like a terrorist
with a stocking over his eye sockets,
cliff cheeks, flattened beak, and slit
tremendous mouth! We freeze and catch our breath.
(What on earth did the last drum say?)
But look – the stage is turning black
with musicians and their instruments!
Now they tune up. Again the tympanist listens,
head flat, to the speech of his drums.
Confetti applause. The music begins.
And now it's his turn: his sticks are raised.
They rattle and blaze. They thump and tap.
Out of great pain, someone is telling a story.
The drums submit; their words are not their own.

The Cave-In

What did he say, that blinded dusty boy,
when he was dug out?
                              – That first the darkness
of the cave-in lay identical, outside and in,
across his eyelids; that the cries
he shrilled met stone and cried back to him
as echoes. He was imprisoned by an entire hill.
So humble and colossal it was, he cried until
the cold stationed in his boots wormed up
to his armpits, and threaded itself on vertebrae
and folded round his belly in a web.
So his tears dried up in convulsive shivers;
the taste of salt and tannin dried out his head.

When he came to, he heard thumps –
his heart, perhaps, or a pavement tamper,
and increasingly nearer, a flutter of water,
a streaming, pounding, a clatter of hoofs
that halted almost on top of him. He knew the advance
of a heavy animal, he smelled sweet grass
on its breath, and acrid hairiness of hide,
before he felt on his ears the bloom
of huge warm lips, tenderly, curiously applied,
and the nudge of damp nostrils on his neck,
and recognized the pushiness of a great beast
used to its own success.
                              He got up (he said)
oh, joyfully, and touched the warm and rounded moleskin
which shut in tons of brilliant flesh,
and felt it glide under his hands, and twitch, ticklish,
till in a gigantic snatch it bolted off
slap into the rock, and there the skull and skeleton
sparked like a lode, or a luminous fossil,
the bones of a horse running; while he heard,
a good way off, the noise of hoofs.

What a horse was doing there, what it meant,
he'd no time to wonder before the rescuers
broke through the rockfall and found him.

I Look for Him Everywhere
(for John)

Walking over the bridge early –
the level of the lake still sunk
   in darkness, and the pale road
barely lifted out of the murk –
   I found a man established
already at the parapet:
   arms out, palms up, fingers fanned,
facing sunrise and a bank of trees
   drab from the last week's heat.
He refused to turn at my footfall.
   I trotted past him like a sheep,
resenting him. This was hardship,
   to be sacrificed to his piety,
the penance in his ritual,
   whatever it was. And instead of dawn,
solitude, and the lake scanned
   for clarity as it reached the sky,
to have this lumber I'd no use for,
   cramming a space meant to be bare! –
I still carry him, arms out, in my mind.

Last month, in Yorkshire, I hunted down
Charles Waterton's Walton Hall,
   pillared and porticoed stone box,
brown paper colour, on its lake.
   Brick houses now look down on it
from the Wakefield side. On the other hill,
   a man ploughed up a great pale square
that grew dark as I watched.
   And I recalled how Waterton
at the end of 1824
   came back here from the Amazon
clad in top hat and old frock coat –
   the pockets ideal for specimens
he was then to label and display
   in glass cases, for visitors.
He made a sanctuary for birds
   out of the Walton woods and lake.

I've read of him, in later years
    he'd only to open his front door
and to extend his arms
    and they converged from every cover
greedy to be fed: bevies at his feet,
    wings on his chest, angel on hat,
two shoulders feathered thick,
    and two arms' worth of birds.
Nothing's left but house and birds –
    widgeon, mallard, teal and coot,
pochard, Canada goose – manoeuvring
    everywhere upon the moat.
His singular gesture folds to rest,
    a butterfly shut in a book.

    Now you're swimming in our pool.
Five laps of the same measure,
    surging with steady uniform stroke,
And you are limber, you emerge.
    The water streams off your grizzled beard
And chest and thighs. You move with towel
    to the luminous shade of the grape arbour,
a man getting on for seventy,
    thinking of this and that, who chuffs
as he rubs the great coloured cloth
    over the verdigris of his flesh.
Out in the sun the water heaves
    in a glittering groping for what's gone.
Did it know what it had as I know it? –
    That nakedness, that transfusion of life?
How easily now belief arrives,
    and worshipfully claims nothing!

Wild Animal Park, San Diego

The rhinoceros stands alone
in a blaze of sun and sand.
His carapace encloses
nothing but absence –
both absence from us and
absence in Africa.

That total armament of his
has no one to impress,
no rhinoceros mate or rival,
not us on the monorail
well-taught by book or film.
'Ah,' we nod, 'ah,'

preparing to glide on,
when below his armour plate
his phallus unsheathes,
big as a bough, naked, rude, red,
and arches to the ground
sun-baked below him.

Goodbye, you dear gazelles,
you shored up trees,
strategic gazebos,
and acres of pretence!
Here's one who thinks on life.
He does not think of us.

The Anarchist

Fénéon passed out most of his pay
to the needy before he reached home.
The rest kept his mother. He married out of pity
a friend whom divorce had compromised,

but maintained his old mistress
and fathered on others two bastard sons.
Bon bourgeois, functionary in the War Office,
but wild for art, he saw the *Illuminations*

of Rimbaud into print and the last verse
of Laforgue; explained Seurat, defended Signac,
hailed Van Gogh. But as critic his chief act
was as an anarchist, reverse

logician, planting a bomb in a crowded café –
a flowerpot bomb, fuse in a hyacinth.
When it went off, a painter lost an eye.
At the trial, Fénéon, impassive as a sphinx,

was acquitted, thanks to innocent friends.
His ironies stayed secret and immune
over the next fifty years, their ends
unimportant, and the self hard as a stone
jiggled in a pocket, kept decently in hand.

Welcome to Mendocino
(to Helen Wheelwright)

1

A tremendous sea, covered with experienced waves.
Crumbling sandstone cliffs, their rock lodes,
their lofty citadels, cut out and marooned.
Seaweed, sea lions, and a set of pelicans
assumed, and the sea passing them by,
the mastering element, the present controller.

But at Mendocino in the last century
the sea looked purely good.
It was what men had to sail on and fish,
and what brought them there in the first place.
The land, too, looked good to mine and sow
and bear crops like other land. Accordingly
men built tall sporty houses in a spacious grid
right on the cove. The grand fronts
they painted pink, green, ochre, blue,
variously lit by the classical Pacific
flashing up the streets' divide.
A stroll through brambles to the shore
brought them a prospect of their neighbour
sea's abundance of colour and detail,
which made them smile, so well they understood.
They went home to add a superfluous fret
of wooden filigrees to eaves and rails,
shingles cut and overlapped like scales on fish,
a delicate fan with glass over a door,
an outside staircase twined like morning glory.

2

The wayfarer runs his Honda up One
some ninety miles, half a day from San Francisco,
just to sleep in an old brass bed and eat breakfast

at one of the new inns of famous Mendocino.
The embroidered sheet turned down so bravely O,
the comforter and three lace pillows, their puffed feathers.

The bathtub with brass taps and lion paws.
The frilly white curtain. Old elephant cypresses
outside, flouncing their own black lace.

Soft as the light, womanly warmth up the mahogany stair.
Coffee, and biscuits baking. A pink appliqued table cloth,
pots of honey and jam, fluted cups, zinnias in a jug.

Silver spoons, knives with bone handles.
China plates wreathed with painted ivy.
The November sun of an old lamp.

*

Pin thin, the innkeeper in her tight blue jeans
    and her sky-blue T-shirt and running shoes.
        Her body bends in an arc like a tossed net

as she stoops to the sweet-breathing old black oven
    and takes out six bread tins
        filled with her own version of zucchini bread.

*

Down through the grid the tourist, touched with fire.
    Sunlight shoots from the experienced sea.
His eyes prickle. His wallet's heavy.
    He'd live here too if he had the money.
He'd thrum with artisans in an atelier,
    ankle-deep in shavings, and make fine things.
He muses from shop to shop and buys expensively,
    the sea at his back, the malign neglected sea.

*

Outside each shop, baskets of geraniums
bright in their crowd of leaves.
A hard wind from the sea. The flowers freshen.
Pretty red petals lick the sidewalk bricks.
But near the dump and its fallen fence
amaryllis as in Greek Sicily,
fleshy amaryllis all in pink,

pink trumpets with a golden tongue
in fullest voice, amaryllis on the fields of Etna,
belles of the ancient world. 'Naked Ladies,'
frowns the prim innkeeper, and slashes off their heads.

3

Unionised labour's gone inland,
gone to the back country,
where the sea is musing and gentle,
far up a river where the tide turns
among trees and fields and mills.
The only knowledge of the sea now
is a slightly moving, tearing bite,
the single symptom of flamboyance.
It's a quiet element for loggers
who float huge trunks in booms
and tether booms to stakes in watery roads
in a basin broad as a town,
and live by the close light of a wood
in houses the colour of old fish,
discarded catch chucked out on a shore.

4

Here come the two Marys in their Toyota.
They've pawed through the merchandise. They're angry.
The stuff's meant for someone with more money.

The shopkeepers, though, wore a nuptial look.
'Goodness, how I loved my mother,' their young men's
little smiles say, as they handed over

a priceless trinket no Mary wanted in her young days
but should be glad of now. But Mary has Mary,
half blind though the one is and the other wheezes.

So what's the sea been up to? – clambering
through briars and paper wrappers down to the cove
where the sea's whimpering, spilling and mowing.

Its quake-strewn ramparts of hewn stone
meet expectation as always and as the Marys do,
since the sea is without necessity,

two-thirds of the earth's surface
but unmarketable; unconserved; not taken into account;
even its fine storms improperly assessed, often,

and, unpredicted, called natural calamities,
as if that nailed them. The sea, admired,
now becomes admirable, and gratis to the point of tears,

like the moose that wandered past the back door once,
in Maine, two calves at heel as big as trucks,
the three of them sauntering into a Mary's life

as if they were safe there for good.
What if the beach tilts against one's eyeball,
coming down, black visor over white metal,

and the other's breath is pelted with grit
until she gasps? The magnificent unplaced desire
at liberty here soon has Marys amused.

The sea becomes their spokesman, mouthing its vowels
between their toes and shoulder-high out there,
it pushes its roars and chirrups into their ears,

it slides wet and heavy into their hands.
And its floor – not like a kitchen floor's
aberration in dirt and stains, but single,

whole. Its stones, now, ovoid and heavy,
that the sea has rolled in the river mouth,
even dried, smell faintly of its breath.

The Marys forage for some that are perfectly round.
They're at home here, with their old measure,
the packaging peeled from the rest of the world.

5

Chaperones with huge beach towels
held out for naked bathers:
in the cool of the garden where the stones will go,
the lords of language with their nets.
Globed silences, placed exactly,
with many a considerate cocking of the head
and standing back to observe the effects.
Bougainvillea, jasmine, ivy, myrtle,
and other jabberers with coloured hats
advance with their paraphernalia of roots
as the garden sways at its anchor,
the perfectly round stones of Mendocino
brought back by the two Marys.

6

The sea grumbles far away, the sea devoid of honour
as it is, gobbling, dangerous, cold, for ever
missing something, it doesn't know what.
'Oh, for God's sake!' it cries, and bellows all night
through the lace curtains of the famous Mendocino inn.
What if the only thing wrong is the moon?
The sea wants its words too, to declare that
it is various and detailed and craves to be looked at,
and gives of itself for ever. It only imagines it is hungry,
full as it must be with continent wolfed.

A Linen Skirt

The flax grew in the field
    So the skirt was tough.
From the first it had the weave
    And hand of field-grown stuff.

But I bit into a peach
    And juice ran over my chin.
I promptly washed the skirt
    But the mark stayed in.

The skirt bleached pale as cream
    And dyed a shade of toast
Except where the juice had fallen
    Where pinkness had set fast.

I cut my finger next
    And drops of blood fell down.
The skirt bleached white as lint
    But the blood turned brown.

Red as a crayfish, then,
    And russet as a bird,
Whatever dyes I chose
    The peach and blood stains showed.

Yet I wear it with delight
    And smile when the colours fade,
Because the weight and weave
    Show something flax has made,

Marked as the palm of my hand
    Where experience is revealed,
Because, I like to think,
    The flax grew in the field.

First the Letters Joined

First the letters joined,
   then words spoke off the page
   in my own voice – strange,
      considering I didn't speak.

I didn't even think,
   yet star worlds alongside
   me sent signals and replied
      to me: inward, outward – one.

A storm about that time
   blew flat our old brick wall.
   The chunks lay on the lawn.
      Instead of wall a view –

narrow back gardens laid
   with paths and cabbage beds,
   huts for tools or hens,
      shrubs, frames, hedges –

like prisoners, calling out.
   It was winter and got dark
   early – my good luck
      to make my way across

unseen, bush by bush,
   under the noise of rain,
   hoping to make them mine
   and stay invisible.

In each terraced house
   a window was lit by then,
   the curtains not yet drawn,
      and families sat at tea

under each fringed lamp –
   parents, girls, boys,
   like us, but still worse
      in that they couldn't see

their own imprisonment –
   my privilege
   whipped across my face –
      even the wallpaper was ugly:

a vestibule of rooms –
   cells – one to a family –
   each a well-lit worn-out certainty.
      Better death! Then came a wall.

Below, the sides of a cutting;
   lamps on a parapet
   showed a tunnel and a set
      of gleaming railway lines.

Far off, a shriek, a tremble,
   then a star world exit,
   a hundred trundling wagons in pursuit,
      out of the ecstatic dark.

And the great whistle again
   piercing and splitting the wet,
   and hope soaring like that
      steam going up to the sky.

Turtle

Old flame-eyes went plunging
   off the log where he sunned himself,
      four leather thumbs stuck out of his carapace,

plunging into the offhand passing water,
   having completely established a
      John D. Rockefeller malevolence –

narrow flame eyes, leather triangular head,
   notably hairless with so much else
      around him furred and feathered and mossed –

only the deep water being quite as nude as he was,
   into which he stirred his thumbs
      in buoyant passage through the thick softness,

the plop of his descent followed by soft
   quiet too – except for the beery bubbly slide
      of the unreflecting big-scaled shell! –

containing an interior undoubtedly beautiful
   when properly scooped out, a carapace melon
      rid of seeds and flesh, Rockefeller bird bath,

delicate white John D. Rockefeller supper
   unplugged and plopped out
      and due to be gloriously served –

while presently a pearly sound
   might swill round the opalescent shell,
      a whirl becoming a gigantic O

opening a tunnel to the airs of heaven
   far-off even now, though bellying out,
      a thimble filled with its power in air

and blown, blown over water now unimpeded,
   a half world supported by proud billows,
      chuckles and suckings of water reverberating

under the keel-less curve of the coracle,
    striking up through the thwart to the soul
        of a pensive creature that steers

and listens to rounded bells welling over water,
    musing: 'Such Apollonian music
        in hospitable deeps away from homely harbour

must come from a pelvis strummed
    or a mandolin pregnant, the musician's hand
        a ravishing cock-a-hoop old man's

lately freed from some crevice
    in that louring outraged mountain yonder;
        for it's so rich, Endymion, it speaks luxury –

money's moons in this wave's hollowed out hand,
    coins jiggled in his pocket – such grief
        in it too, Endymion, for when his means are gone:

meanwhile this thought world, hemisphere
    that's only imagined empty, it weighs
        heavy with millionaire ideas, like seed pearls.'

And loosening all those heavy tresses of hers,
    she stood upright, and waves took the shell headlong
        and bore her cresting to a scrap of sand.

Nicholas

Dead Nicholas
smiles out of the photograph
on the stairs of the borrowed house
and I recall that when he was
a boy, put to bed, he'd smiling
stealthily reappear
His steps and voice
are now a man's default

though too he's ever-present,
a dislodged marble
dropping daily from stair to stair
past the eternal photograph
of himself once smiling
out through the front door
and into the street

a wrecker's ball
hauled back on its chain
and swung against a building
till the windows pop
and the frames collapse
and remaining walls let go

The Two-Man Saw

'You are cutting down a tree!'
Sagacious, in fresh cotton,
she advanced among the furious geese
to the edge of the lawn and the bald old elm
we were at work on.

'Do you know how to cut down a tree?'
We paused while she readied advice,
and over the clangour of geese
nodded as gay as we could, once more
a colonial couple in the wilderness,

and bent to the great Victorian saw,
one on each handle, rowing the huge
blade between us, one to the other,
as she watched, and the geese
extended their black nibs and hissed.

We were coated in sweat, you and I,
floured with sawdust, our eyes
starting and streaming with heat,
but how could we miss the sweet sap smell
that rose from the saw's stroke,

as of saint's blood, fragrant, incorruptible,
or not feel the elm's veer on its ropes
while, powered with regret, we sawed like maniacs,
and the saw bound, and came free,
and bound? And the instant before the elm

yielded and swayed down to the ground,
boughs a-crack, an unknown miraculous
virtue became manifest among us,
as if a hero had died
in an epic, in front of frightened squaddies.